Another View from My Deck

Haikus Inspired by Nature

All poetry contained in this work is the original work of the author.

Published by St. Petersburg Press

St. Petersburg, FL

www.stpetersburgpress.com

Design and composition by St. Petersburg Press and Pablo Guidi

Cover design by St. Petersburg Press and Pablo Guidi, photo by Timothy Huff

Print ISBN: 978-1-940300-92-4

eBook ISBN: 978-1-940300-93-1

First Edition

Another View from My Deck

Haikus Inspired by Nature

Timothy Huff

This book is dedicated to my late parents Jeanne and Joe Huff. When I was 6 years old, they built our family home on the side of a mountain. The woods around our home gave me my first appreciation of nature.

#37

Rain drop on a leaf

So clear clean and reflective

Nature gazing ball

#38

Cute heather flowers

Beautiful small nature's rug

Delicate and sweet

#39
There dark cloud goes by
Quick cooling moment of shade
The dark cloud goes on

#40
Sweet gift this morning
Delicate soft pink dove egg
Baby bird to come

#41
Cute baby lizard
So prehistoric looking
Quickly off he goes

#42

Sweet little wild finch

Here there everywhere he goes

Constantly moving

#43
Thick morning sea fog
Mother Nature's damp wet veil
Hey are you in there?

#44

Sprinkler time! Fun time!

Birds come and whizz through water

Wet cool refreshing

#45
Summer solstice bright
The longest day of the year
Warm energy plus

#46
Cocoon under leaf
Inside butterfly surprise
Patiently waiting

#47

Such lovely bird songs
Look at me I am handsome
Mocking birds mating

#48

Sparrow commotion

Chasing, flying, much squawking

Three curious squirrels

#49

Pretty orchid bloom

First one of the spring season

Many more to come

#50

Yellow and black stripes

So striking on porter weed

Zebra butterfly

#51
Green metallic bee
Hovers on new pink orchid
Sweet scented pollen

#52
Oh look one, two, three
Swallow tails in backyard flight
Thank you dutchman's pipe

#53

Single orchid bloom
Rich burgundy and yellow
Regal but alone

#54

Found jasmine snowflake
Hung by spider's lone web string.
Breeze spins single bloom

#55

Sky and leaves combine

Nature's own kaleidoscope

Blue green through the trees

#56

Last gardenia bloom

Now spring fades into summer

Savoring the scent

#57

Cooler nights begin

Moon stars appear earlier

Oh autumn is here

#58

White queen of the night
Exotic alien like bloom
Night moth sweet delight

#59

Squirrel sits on fence

Pulls down beauty berry branch

Yummy morning snack

#60

Birds squirrels flowers

Sweet gifts from mother nature

So very thankful

#61
Wispy clouds up high
Long white feathers in the sky
Stunning against blue

#62

Little lizard play

I am king of the mountain

Chase others away

#63
Little baby dove
Such protective mother's love
Cuddled in the nest

#64
Orange beauty looms
Canna up through schefflera
Lone phoenix rising

#65
Rain drop on yellow
Refreshed allamanda bloom
Nature's nourishment

#66
Chilly quiet night
Bright full moon in the still sky
November halo

#67

Squawking in the sky
Wild parrots flying over
Brilliant green with black

#68

Little opossum run

Night of eating fun is done

Off to daytime sleep

#69

Winter cold morning
Peanuts and seeds to comfort
Sympathy for all

#70

Cold chilly morning

Squirrels curled up in their beds

Furry tail blankets

#71
First comes the mister
chirp chirp there is the missus
Happy cardinals

#72

Stillness of the night

Quiet peace across all lands

Winter solstice here

Timothy Huff, a Binghamton, New York transplant, is a lover of nature and sunshine - which brought him to our beautiful St. Petersburg some 30+ years ago. He lives his Florida dream with husband Randy and his dog, Toby.

A custom window treatment designer by profession, the COVID crisis brought out his inner poet, sharing Haikus with online friends.

Tim joyfully shares collected observations of the life he loves with you...

www.haikutim.com